THE
Signature
FISH STORY

"7-UNIQUE
CHRIST-CENTERED "FISH"
TECHNIQUES TO A
FULFILLING RELATIONSHIP"

Marital Inspiration Organization by _____
Vineyard & Co. LLC

Copyright © 2021 by Marital Inspiration Organization by Vineyard & Co. LLC Updated 2021, 2022, 2023, 2024. All rights reserved.

Title: The Signature Fish Story

Published by: Marital Inspiration Organization by Vineyard & Co. LLC

Author: Montoya Williams

Unauthorized Use Prohibited. No part of this book may be reproduced, transmitted, or utilized in any form or by any means, electronic or mechanical, including photocopying, recording, or any information storage and retrieval system,
without the prior written permission of the publisher.

For permissions, please contact:

Marital Inspiration Organization by Vineyard & Co. LLC

[info@maritalinspirations.org]

ISBN: 979-8-9916301-7-7

Unless otherwise indicated, all Scripture quotations are taken from the King James Version (KJV).

Printed in the United States of America

Dedication

I dedicate this Book with heartfelt gratitude to our children's children and everyone God has brought into my life through this divine ministry. May the wisdom shared here inspire and guide you toward a fulfilling and grace-filled relationship anchored in the love and obedience of our Lord and Savior, Jesus Christ.

Marital Inspiration Organization
by
Vineyard & Co. LLC

Please visit our Website:
https://maritalinspirations.org

Appreciations

In appreciating "*The Signature Fish Story*, I express deep gratitude to God for answering my prayers and blessing me with a wonderful husband.

I reflect on the journey I've experienced—from the longing for marriage to the joy of a fulfilling, Christ-centered relationship. Acknowledging God's steadfast faithfulness, I am grateful for His guidance and how He has aligned my path with His purpose. This transformative course has influenced and guided my work with Marital Inspiration Organization by Vineyard & Co. LLC.

I also extend heartfelt thanks to my wonderful husband, appreciating him for his unconditional love and unwavering support and for always having my back through every challenge. His dedication and partnership have genuinely reflected God's love in my life, strengthening my marriage and inspiring my commitment to helping others on their marital journeys. Through this expression of gratitude, I celebrate both the divine and earthly love that has shaped my life and my mission to support others in their relationships.

TABLE OF CONTENTS

INTRODUCTION ... 00
Introduction To:
The "Signature Fish Story"

CATCH THE FISH ... 01
Acknowledge Your Struggles

SCALE THE FISH ... 02
Uncover Your Struggles

GUT THE FISH ... 03
Remove Your Struggles

WASH THE FISH ... 04
Clean-Up Your Struggles

SEASON THE FISH ... 05
Prepare To Receive ...

COOK THE FISH ... 06
Make Ready To Receive

SERVE THE FISH ... 07
Become Ready To Receive ...

https://maritalinspirations.org

Introduction

Welcome to "*The Signature Fish Story,*" a transformative guide designed to help you prepare for, enter, and nurture a fulfilling relationship through the grace of our Lord and Savior, Jesus Christ. In this book, you'll discover a unique approach to relationship readiness using a simple yet profound Seven-Step "Fish" Technique: The Catch, The Scale, The Gut, The Wash, The Season, The Cook, and The Serve. These steps symbolize a profound personal growth and preparation journey, metaphorically preparing "Your Fish" to be presented at its finest.

As you journey through this guide, you will meet the relatable characters, "Mr. & Mrs. Right." They represent non-fictional experiences from real-life struggles, triumphs, and spiritual revelations. Their stories will illuminate the path to a Christ-centered relationship, blending the richness of narrative with the practicality of lived experiences. Through their journeys, you'll find relatable moments, spiritual insights, and actionable steps that resonate deeply with your life and aspirations.

Drawing from my experiences as a woman who has embraced both singleness and the joy of marriage, I'm eager to share the lessons and encouragement that have enriched my journey. I speak from the heart of someone who once yearned for marriage and now embraces the blessings of a loving partnership. Centered on Christ, I demonstrate that faith is the key to cultivating a meaningful and lasting relationship. This book is a heartfelt invitation to allow God to guide you in presenting your best self. With God's grace, you will learn how to approach your relationship with renewed purpose and devotion.

As the founder of Marital Inspiration Organization by
Vineyard & Co. LLC,
I hope to support and encourage you in your journey through our educational coaching and consulting services
and the accessible inspiration available
on our website, https://maritalinspirations.org.

Thank you for joining me. May this book guide and inspire you as you prepare to serve your most authentic and cherished self.

Chapter 1

The Catch

For years, she had been waiting for her "Mr. Right," the man who would bring completeness to her life. In her small town, she found comfort in her routine as an elementary school teacher's aide but longed for deeper companionship.

Every summer, her mornings started at the local bookstore, where she loved curling up with a novel and a cup of coffee. On Wednesday, a tall, handsome stranger walked in, catching her attention. Their eyes met, and she felt a flutter in her chest. He approached her, asking if he could join her at her table since the other seats were taken. Surprised but charmed, she welcomed him.

He introduced himself as the new basketball coach at Glen High School. They chatted easily, enjoying their connection. Before long, they agreed to meet again the next day.

The following day, she felt excited as he arrived with her favorite coffee. They talked about their jobs and shared their love for teaching. Their chemistry grew, and they exchanged phone numbers.

By Friday, after spending time getting to know each other, their coffee dates had become the highlight of the week. Mr. Right had learned enough about Ms. Right to feel comfortable suggesting a visit to the pond she used to go to with her grandfather—a place filled with cherished memories. Ms. Right happily agreed, and together, they decided to turn their "catch" into an evening dinner date at her home.

The next day, they met at the pond, excitement crackling in the crisp air. Their easy chatter and the thrill of catching their first fish made the hours fly by. By the time they wrapped up, they had finally caught a fish big enough for
their first dinner date.

Later that evening, she returned home to prepare the fish, her mind drifting to her past. Memories she thought she'd buried began to resurface—moments of joy and pain. As she prepared the fish, she realized this dinner meant more than just a meal; it was a chance to confront her hidden scars.

As the sun set, she dressed in a beautiful purple dress and adorned herself with pearls from her beloved grandmother. Feeling a mix of excitement and self-consciousness, she knew deep down it felt right.

Just before seven, she lit candles, creating a warm atmosphere. When the doorbell rang, her heart raced. She opened the door to find Mr. Right, tall and handsome in a suit. They paused, taking in the moment's significance.
"Come in," she said softly.

As he entered, he couldn't help but admire her efforts. "You look stunning. And the dinner smells fantastic," he said warmly. She blushed, her cheeks glowing as she led him to the table, where everything was set with thoughtful care.

At the center of the table was a beautifully engraved silver platter, passed down from her grandmother—a family heirloom that added a touch of elegance to the moment.

Once they sat at the table, Mr. Right led them in a heartfelt prayer. After the prayer,

At first glance, the fish looked beautifully prepared—its golden exterior and savory aroma were enticing.

But as Mr. Right took a closer look, he realized something was off. The fish hadn't been scaled or cleaned—in fact, the guts were still inside.

Concern flickered in his eyes as he gently asked, "Did something happen while preparing the fish?"

Taking a deep breath, Ms. Right looked at him with vulnerability. "You seem like the man I've been praying for, but I feel like this fish," she said, her voice trembling. "On the outside, I look perfect at first glance, but there are flaws underneath…"

Tears welled in her eyes as she began to share her struggles—her father's absence, her mother's instability, her early marriage and painful divorce, and the heartache of losing custody of her daughter. "I'm broken and don't know how to fix myself," she admitted, her words heavy with emotion.

He reached across the table, taking her hand. "You are beautiful to me," he said gently. "I appreciate your honesty. I have a similar story."

He shared his own journey: raised by grandparents, a troubled marriage after a pro football career, and the challenges of divorce. "Counseling changed my life, and now I co-parent my kids healthily," he explained.

After their heartfelt exchange and realizing the dinner she prepared was not edible, he suggested going out for dinner instead, sensing their growing connection. She agreed, and they spent the evening enjoying their meal, laughing, and deepening their bond.

On the drive back, Mr. Right felt inspired by his faith. As they approached her home, he asked, "Would you join me for worship tomorrow? I'd love for you to experience my church." She smiled and accepted.

Then, he opened her car door and escorted her inside. The night air felt charged with promise as they hugged. "Goodnight," they whispered, lingering in the embrace before parting ways. He walked back to his car, grateful for the woman he was getting to know.

On Sunday, the service was uplifting, and afterward, they shared lunch, continuing to connect spiritually. Mr. Right introduced the counselor to Ms. Right via phone, and they later met at the counselor's home for Ms. Right to share her story.

After hearing about how the night had unfolded, especially how Ms. Right vulnerably expressed her emotions around the fish dinner she had prepared, the counselor was inspired to create The Virtual Liberating Marital Experience.

The counselor chose the fish technique for her program, deeply moved by the metaphor Ms. Right had shared earlier with Mr. Right. Ms. Right had compared herself to a fish—appearing beautiful on the outside yet struggling with deep internal challenges that needed healing. This powerful story resonated with the counselor, who saw the fish metaphor as the perfect framework to guide Ms. Right through her transformative healing process.

The counselor explained how each phase of the fish preparation would symbolize different stages of growth and healing.

1. Catching the Fish is about acknowledging your struggles—coming to terms with the challenges you've faced.
2. Scaling the Fish involves uncovering your struggles—digging deeper to understand the root of your pain.
3. Gutting the Fish is about removing your struggles—releasing the burdens and emotional weight that have held you back.
4. Washing the Fish is to clean up your struggles—cleansing and healing from the emotional wounds.
5. After cleaning and healing, Seasoning the Fish represents preparing to receive—getting ready to embrace new possibilities and opportunities.
6. Cooking the Fish is about making room to receive—creating space in your life for new blessings and experiences.
7. Finally, Serving the Fish on a Beautiful Silver Platter symbolizes becoming ready to receive fully, prepared to share your healed and whole self with others.

Ms. Right felt a deep sense of clarity and hope as the counselor outlined this structured approach. They agreed that Ms. Right would meet the counselor at her home Monday through Friday for lunch, working through one phase each week.

On Saturdays, Mr. Right would be invited to join them for lunch, allowing him to review the week's work, offer feedback, and walk alongside Ms. Right as she embarked on this new journey.

The supportive, structured plan gave Ms. Right a renewed sense of purpose and excitement for what lay ahead.

The chapter ends with warm goodbyes and promises for the counselor and Ms. Right to start on Monday with "The Scale" of the Fish.

Chapter 2

The Scale

Monday: Confronting Abandonment

Ms. Right arrived at the Counselor's home feeling both excited and nervous. After a lovely lunch, they settled on the couch, and the Counselor created a warm atmosphere to begin their session.

"Can you share when those moments with your father happened and describe how they affected you emotionally?" the Counselor inquired softly.

Taking a deep breath, Ms. Right shared, "My father left when I was young. I've always felt abandoned, and it's hard for me to trust anyone. My mother said he struggled with addiction, but his absence has left deep scars."

Tears filled her eyes as she spoke. "I constantly fear that everyone I care about will leave me, and that fear haunts me."

The Counselor nodded. "Acknowledging this pain is essential for healing."

After a deep conversation about how her past abandonment shaped her fears, they wrapped up the session feeling positive about the progress.

Tuesday: Navigating Maternal Neglect

The next day, Ms. Right returned, ready to explore her relationship with her mother.

"My mother was never really there for me when I was young," she confessed. "She focused on her partners instead of me. I often felt worthless and unloved."

Tears streamed down her face. "I felt isolated and like no one truly cared."

The Counselor offered comfort. "Opening up about these feelings is a significant step toward healing."

They spoke at length about how her mother's neglect affected her self-worth and relationships, and after a reflective discussion, they ended the session pleased with the day's work.

Wednesday: Facing Marital Abuse

On Wednesday, Ms. Right came back, ready to discuss her ex-husband.

"My marriage was toxic. I faced mental, verbal, and physical abuse.

He isolated me from friends and family, making me feel utterly alone," she shared, her voice trembling. "He called me names and threatened me. I felt trapped and dependent on him," she admitted, breaking down.

The Counselor listened with compassion. "Facing these truths takes bravery. Continue processing these emotions."

After a heartfelt conversation, they concluded the session with a heavy but hopeful heart.

Thursday: The Strain of Maternal Separation

On Thursday, they focused on her relationship with her daughter. "My depression affected our bond," she said, tears in her eyes. "I hid the abuse from her to protect her. My ex-husband turned her against me."

"I felt lost and unable to reach out for help," she added, sobbing.

The Counselor embraced her. "It's vital to uncover this pain for your healing. Stay hopeful for the future."

As the counselor continued to offer words of comfort, Ms. Right found solace in her understanding, and they wrapped up the evening on a hopeful note.

Friday: Examining Self-Worth

On Friday, Ms. Right arrived determined to explore her feelings about herself.

"I've always felt worthless and sought validation," she said softly. "The shame I carry is overwhelming."

As the session continued, Ms. Right shared more about her struggles with self-esteem and the deep-rooted fears that had shaped her decisions and relationships. She opened up about moments in her life when she felt invisible and unworthy, expressing her longing to break free from these feelings.

The Counselor listened intently, offering reassurance and guidance. "You've made incredible progress this week. Acknowledging these struggles is liberating."

Feeling a sense of freedom, Ms. Right said, "I feel like I'm on the brink of a breakthrough."

The Counselor smiled encouragingly. "Next week, we'll start 'The Gut' phase, where we'll work on removing these struggles."

Before leaving, Ms. Right shared how much she appreciated the process.

The Counselor reminded her that Mr. Right would join them the next day to review the week's progress.

Ms. Right felt a renewed sense of hope, knowing she had his support on this transformative journey.

She left feeling empowered and ready for the next steps, looking forward to sharing the experience with Mr. Right on Saturday.

Saturday: Evaluating Progress and Preparing for Next Steps

Mr. Right and Ms. Right arrived at the counselor's house as planned on Saturday for lunch. After enjoying a meal together, the counselor invited both of them out to her lovely patio, where she had set up a laptop for them to review The Scale phase of The Virtual Liberating Marital Experience.

She asked them to take their time, review the materials, and share their thoughts on how they felt about the phase.

After some time, they returned inside, and Mr. Right spoke first. "I'm impressed with how you've structured everything. It makes so much sense. The Scale phase reminded me of the importance of acknowledging and uncovering our struggles before moving forward. "I'm excited about where this is heading."

Ms. Right added, "I really resonated with the idea of 'scaling' the fish. It felt symbolic to dig deep and honestly face what I've been avoiding. It wasn't easy, but it gave me a sense of clarity.
I'm grateful for this process.
I think it will help me heal in ways I didn't expect."

As the evening came to a close, Mr. Right and Ms. Right thanked the Counselor for her guidance and left together, reflecting on the progress made and the journey still ahead.

Sunday: A Day of Worship and Rest

Sunday became a cherished routine for Mr. and Ms. Right as they attended worship together, strengthening their bond.

Afterward, they enjoyed a lovely lunch and felt grateful for their journey.

As the day ended, they reflected on the transformative week and the path ahead, feeling a sense of peace.

Chapter 3

The Gut

Monday: Uncovering the Roots of Abandonment

Ms. Right arrived at the Counselor's home, feeling a mix of anticipation and weight. After lunch, they settled on the couch.

The Counselor explained that this phase, "The Gut," was about understanding the emotional burdens from her past.

"Why do you think your father left?" the Counselor asked gently.

Ms. Right hesitated, then replied, "I think he left because his father was absent. He didn't know how to be a dad."

The Counselor nodded. "Take a deep breath and sit with that." As Ms. Right reflected, the Counselor continued, "Why do you think he chose addiction?"

"He turned to drugs because he was fighting his demons," she said, pain evident in her voice.

Ms. Right continued to share more about her memories of her father, releasing emotions she had buried for years.

The Counselor encouraged her to rest with these thoughts as they wrapped up the session.

Tuesday: Understanding Maternal Choices

The next day, Ms. Right returned, ready to explore her mother's choices.

"Why do you think your mother was more available to her partners than you?" the Counselor asked.

"She was looking for the love she never got from her father," Ms. Right replied, sadness filling her voice.

The Counselor offered her support. "Allow that truth to settle."

Then the Counselor asked, "Why do you think your mother allowed abuse in her relationships?"

"I think she believed it was the price for financial security," Ms. Right said, trembling.

Ms. Right shared more about her childhood experiences, opening up about the pain she carried from watching her mother suffer.

"Let's pause here," the Counselor suggested as they prepared to close the session.

Wednesday: Revealing the Source of Marital Abuse

On Wednesday, they moved back to the couch.

The Counselor asked, "Why do you think your ex-husband abused you?"

Ms. Right took a deep breath. "He had resentment towards his mother and took it out on me. He needed control, and I wasn't perfect in our arguments."

"Let those thoughts settle," the Counselor encouraged.

"Why do you think he used finances to control you?" the Counselor continued.

"I wasn't attracted to him initially; I was interested in his money. He made sure I depended on him, and when I tried to leave, he used finances against me," Ms. Right explained.

Before ending the evening, Ms. Right shared more about how those experiences had shaped her view of relationships, feeling both raw and relieved.

"Let's rest now," the Counselor said, sensing the weight of her words.

Thursday: The Impact of Parental Conflict on the Child

When Ms. Right arrived on Thursday, the atmosphere felt heavy.

The Counselor asked, "Why do you think your daughter turned against you?"

"I didn't want her to grow up without a father, so I encouraged their bond, even while suffering. But I became so depressed that I couldn't be the mother she needed," she admitted.

The Counselor showed compassion.
"You've faced a difficult truth. "

Ms. Right opened up further, sharing painful memories of how her daughter's rejection deepened her feelings of inadequacy.

They ended the evening on a note of reflection, acknowledging the courage it took to confront such truths.

Friday: Breaking the Cycle of Self-Worth

On Friday, Ms. Right returned, feeling the weight of the week.

The Counselor gently asked, "Why do you think you were affected by your parents' mistakes?"

"I didn't feel worthy enough to make better choices," she replied softly.
"My father's absence made me feel unlovable, and my mother's neglect reinforced that."

The Counselor moved closer, offering warmth. "You've carried so much. It's time to give yourself grace."

Ms. Right felt a sense of relief. "I didn't know how to love myself."

Ms. Right continued to share more deeply about how these feelings had impacted her self-worth and choices.

They agreed to continue the next day, with Mr. Right joining them to review the week's progress.

Saturday: Evaluating Progress and Preparing for Next Steps

Mr. and Ms. Right arrived together, feeling strong in their unity.

After lunch, they went to the patio for the Virtual Experience.

Then, they returned to share their observations. Mr. Right spoke first. "I'm proud of how you've faced this, Ms. Right."

"It wasn't easy, but it was necessary for healing," she said.

The Counselor agreed. "Next week, we'll start 'The Wash' phase to clean up the struggles."

The Counselor shared the details of the phase, and they concluded the session feeling ready to move forward with hope.

Sunday: A Day of Worship and Rest

Mr. and Ms. Right spent Sunday in worship, feeling uplifted by their shared experience. After lunch, they returned home, embracing a sense of peace as they prepared for the week ahead.

Chapter 4

The Wash

Monday: Confronting Life's Struggles and Finding Healing Through Christ

After Ms. Right arrived, they finished lunch and settled on the couch. The Counselor reminded her that the fourth phase of their experience was "The Wash" of the Fish, symbolizing cleaning up life's struggles and moving forward.

The Counselor shared that, moving forward, they would begin each day by opening in prayer to invite God's presence and guidance into their journey, and they would close each evening with prayer to reflect, seek peace, and prepare their hearts for continued healing. This approach, she explained, would center their work on Christ and allow His grace to lead them through the process. Ms. Right gracefully agreed.

After prayer, the Counselor began by sharing her personal story of struggle and how it ultimately brought her closer to Christ. She emphasized that healing often comes from those who offer wisdom and help reclaim power from difficult situations. She recounted a pivotal moment from her youth—a small lie that snowballed into feelings of guilt and shame, which eventually drove her to seek solace in Christ. She explained how she found comfort through prayer and scripture and began to let go of the anger she held toward those who had hurt her.

The Counselor also reflected on her journey of mentorship. One of her mentors introduced her to a deeper understanding of Christ, helping her to approach life's challenges with maturity and grace. Through this guidance, she learned the importance of investing in wisdom and support that would shape her future.

As they continued their conversation, Ms. Right felt inspired. She shared how she longed for guidance to get to know Christ more intimately, to forgive those who had wronged her, and to discover her true self. She also expressed her need for help in preparing for shared custody of her daughter and remarrying for the right reasons.

The Counselor listened with care and compassion, affirming Ms. Right's desire to grow and heal. She suggested that throughout the week, they would continue discussing these essential topics in greater depth, offering reassurance that this journey would bring clarity and hope. Before concluding the evening, the Counselor led them in prayer.

Tuesday: Deepening Your Relationship with Christ and Forgiving the Past

The following day, after lunch, they began the session with prayer, and Ms. Right and the Counselor continued their conversation. The Counselor emphasized the importance of reading and applying God's Word to build a relationship with Christ. She shared how forgiveness had brought her spiritual freedom, allowing her to pray with a clear heart.

They explored Ms. Right's feelings about her father's abandonment and how it impacted her sense of worth. The Counselor encouraged her to forgive him and understand that his struggles weren't her fault.

Ms. Right committed to showing up differently in future relationships, focusing on her identity in Christ.

They also discussed Ms. Right's relationship with her mother and the impact of her mother's struggles.

Understanding these dynamics made Ms. Right feel lighter and more determined to be a better mother.

After this, they addressed her past relationship with her ex-husband.

Ms. Right took accountability for marrying for the wrong reasons and staying in an abusive situation. She vowed to prioritize her and her child's well-being, ensuring they would only live in loving environments.

They ended the session with prayer, and Ms. Right left feeling hopeful.

Wednesday: Embracing Wholeness

On Wednesday, Ms. Right arrived feeling hopeful. The Counselor praised her progress, prayed and introduced the concept of embracing wholeness. She shared her transformation, emphasizing the importance of loving and respecting oneself.

The Counselor explained that knowing one's unique identity in Christ helps in healing. She encouraged Ms. Right to embrace her individuality and focus on her strengths rather than past mistakes.

She discussed the importance of being content in singleness, enjoying her own company, and understanding self-worth before seeking relationships.

The Counselor highlighted how her growing relationship with God led her to find validation in Him rather than others.

For homework, the Counselor encouraged Ms. Right to spend time in the Word, reflect on her journey, and embrace her own company. As they ended with prayer, Ms. Right felt renewed and excited to continue her journey toward healing and purpose.

Thursday: Preparing for Shared Custody and Purposeful Remarriage

Ms. Right arrived at the Counselor's house, eager to enter into prayer and discuss how to prepare for shared custody of her daughter and to remarry for the right reasons. Their bond had grown, making this meeting feel significant.

After a light lunch, they settled on the couch. The Counselor acknowledged Ms. Right's progress, noting that her decision to deepen her relationship with Christ was the first step in preparing for custody. She encouraged Ms. Right to pray for guidance and trust that God would help her find the right resources.

The Counselor reminded Ms. Right that her journey was also for her daughter. Her child needed to see the strength and peace Ms. Right had found in Christ. They prayed together, lifting Ms. Right's daughter, ex-husband, and wife, filling the room with hope.

Next, they discussed how to prepare for remarriage. The Counselor explained that the previous phases of their experience—Acknowledging, Uncovering, Removing, and now, Cleansing—helped create a foundation for transformation. Ms. Right should approach new relationships from a place of wholeness, reflecting the positive changes she has made.

The Counselor advised her to let her conversations reflect the joy and peace she had gained through Christ.

Ms. Right felt a surge of affirmation and gratitude for the Counselor's guidance.

The discussion shifted to the importance of dating with purpose. The Counselor shared her experiences, highlighting the need to align with someone who genuinely values a relationship with Christ and personal growth. She emphasized the importance of setting boundaries and recognizing when to avoid unhealthy situations.

Feeling transformed and ready, Ms. Right expressed her excitement about embracing the future. The Counselor praised her progress, prayed, and made plans to meet again the next day.

As Ms. Right left, her heart felt light, eager to share her gratitude with Mr. Right.

When she called him, Mr. Right was moved by her transformation and expressed his desire to take her on another date.

Ms. Right responded warmly, "I'd like to go on another date, Mr. Right.

" However, before they could confirm any details, she ended the call, leaving the next steps open for further reflection.

Friday: Overcoming Limitations and Preparing for Blessings
On Friday, after opening their session with prayer and grounding themselves in faith, Ms. Right eagerly shared that Mr. Right had asked her on a date. The Counselor responded positively, expressing how good that was for Ms. Right's growth. Then, the Counselor, feeling led by the Spirit, introduced a new concept for the upcoming phase: "Season of the Fish," a time of self-care and preparing to be received.

The Counselor encouraged Ms. Right to allow her to suggest a date for her and Mr. Right, which they would discuss when he joined the session the following day to review "The Wash of the Fish." If Mr. Right agreed, Ms. Right was to spend Monday through Thursday reflecting on the work they had done so far. Then, on Friday, she was to meet the Counselor bright and early at her home for breakfast, where they would proceed with a full day dedicated to self-care, during which Ms. Right would invest in herself.

As they continued their session, they discussed the issues Ms. Right had been facing, including feelings of scarcity. The Counselor reminded her that God calls us to live abundantly and encouraged her to trust in His provision. They also explored codependency and how it can distract from God's will. The Counselor urged Ms. Right to place her hope in God alone, emphasizing that fear should not dictate her choices.

With newfound clarity, Ms. Right recognized the fears she had been holding onto and felt ready to release them. The Counselor encouraged her to focus on the journey ahead rather than looking back.

Ms. Right felt an overwhelming sense of excitement at this new direction and happily agreed to the plan.

The Counselor presented her with an itinerary titled "The Season: Prepare to Receive," which included daily prayer, meditation, and the full day of self-care scheduled for Friday.

Excited and ready for the next steps, Ms. Right agreed to begin with daily prayer and meditation, looking forward to the transformation to come.

They ended in prayer, agreeing for Ms. Right to return the following day with Mr. Right to review
"The Wash" of the Experience.

Saturday: Celebrating Transformation and Embracing New Opportunities

They began the session with an opening prayer, inviting Mr. Right to join them in this spiritual moment. After reviewing the experience, Mr. Right shared how transformative the Wash phase had been for Ms. Right and acknowledged the significant progress she had made. Ms. Right smiled in agreement, feeling the weight of her growth.

As the conversation continued, the Counselor turned to Mr. Right and spoke directly to him, "Instead of coming to the experimental session next Saturday, I'd like to propose an idea. Why don't you take Ms. Right on a second dinner date? This will give her the time she needs to reflect and prepare for a special day of self-care during the upcoming week. You can then experience the beauty of her transformation when you share that Saturday together."

Mr. Right, excited by the suggestion, asked if Ms. Right was open to it, and she happily agreed.

The Counselor reminded Ms. Right to reflect deeply from Monday through Thursday, and they agreed to meet bright and early on Friday for breakfast at the Counselor's house, where they would explore a carefully crafted self-care itinerary.

With their plans in place, they closed the evening in prayer, excited for the week ahead and feeling hopeful about the growth and transformation to come.

Sunday: A Day of Worship and Rest

On Sunday, Ms. Right and Mr. Right attended church together, enjoying the uplifting service and reflecting on their journey.

Afterward, they shared dinner, appreciating each other's company while acknowledging how much they had grown. They ended the evening at their own homes, honoring the need for rest.

Chapter 5

The Season

Monday: Laying the Foundation

As Monday began, Ms. Right was excited, viewing this week as a journey to embrace the woman God created her to be. She committed to starting each day with prayer, meditation, and studying the Word of God. These quiet moments prepared her heart for transformation.

Each morning, Ms. Right woke early to read the Bible and spend time in God's presence. These moments deepened her understanding of her identity in Christ. She reflected on Psalm 139:14 kjv, which says, "I will praise thee; for I am fearfully and wonderfully made: marvelous are thy works; and that my soul knoweth right well." The verse reminded her that she was cherished and whole in God's eyes, which gave her strength to move forward.

Tuesday: Embracing Singleness

That evening, Ms. Right also meditated on Isaiah 41:10 kjv, which says:

"Fear thou not; for I am with thee: be not dismayed; for I am thy God: I will strengthen thee; yea, I will help thee; yea, I will uphold thee with the right hand of my righteousness."

This verse reminded her that she was never alone.
Even in her singleness,
God was with her, strengthening and guiding her.
It gave her the courage to trust His timing and embrace this season as a sacred time to deepen her relationship with Him.

Wednesday: The Power of God's Love

On Wednesday, Ms. Right spent the day to herself, reflecting on all that she had learned so far. Through prayer, meditation, and studying God's Word, she allowed His love to fill her heart and renew her spirit.

As she reflected, she meditated on Jeremiah 29:11 (NIV), which says, "For I know the plans I have for you," declares the Lord, "plans to prosper you and not to harm you, plans to give you hope and a future."

This verse reassured her that God's love was intentional and purposeful. It reminded her that even in seasons of waiting, His plans were for her good—to prosper her, to give her hope, and to prepare her for the future, He had lovingly designed.

She journaled her thoughts, expressing gratitude for the ways God was shaping her heart and teaching her to trust His timing. She wrote about how His plans were far greater than anything she could imagine and how His love was sustaining her through this transformative season.

Throughout the day, Ms. Right used her quiet moments to seek God's wisdom and guidance. That evening, she closed the day in prayer, thanking Him for His unwavering love, the hope He was filling her with, and the future He was preparing for her. In her heart, she felt renewed confidence that God's plans were leading her toward abundant joy and fulfillment.

Thursday: Releasing Old Wounds

Thursday became a day of breakthrough for Ms. Right. Through prayer and time in the Word, she surrendered past hurts, shame, and fears. The Counselor encouraged her to release these burdens and to trust in God's validation over any human judgment.

That evening, Ms. Right prayed, thanking God for the renewal she was experiencing. She reflected on Isaiah 43:18-19 kjv, which says, "Remember ye not the former things, neither consider the things of old. Behold, I will do a new thing; now it shall spring forth; shall ye not know it? I will even make a way in the wilderness, and rivers in the desert."

This scripture reminded her of God's ability to bring new life and purpose out of any situation.

With each day, Ms. Right felt her heart being prepared for the blessings and opportunities ahead.

Friday: A Day of Self-Care

Friday arrived with excitement. Ms. Right awoke early, knowing her self-care day was about spiritual renewal, not just pampering. After breakfast with the Counselor, they began a day focused on self-love.

Manicure and Pedicure

At the salon, Ms. Right felt nurtured. Each stroke of polish symbolized her letting go of emotional burdens and embracing the newness God offered.

Lunch

Over lunch, they shared a healthy meal and discussed Ms. Right's growth and the importance of nourishing both body and soul.

Spa Day

At the spa, Ms. Right relaxed deeply. As tension melted away, she imagined releasing her past pains, inviting God's peace into her life.

Salon Session

Next, a hair makeover reflected her inner renewal. The Counselor reminded her that this transformation was about embracing her true self.

Shopping

Shopping was joyful, Ms. Right chose clothes that made her feel confident and celebrated her growth.

Dinner Alone

The day concluded with Ms. Right dining alone. She realized that being single meant being whole, so she savored each bite, appreciating her own company.

Saturday: Preparing for a Second Date

On Saturday, Ms. Right felt transformed and centered. After prayer, she looked forward to her date with Mr. Right. She chose an outfit that made her feel radiant, honoring herself.

Mr. Right's Preparation

Mr. Right was calm yet excited. He saw this date as a meaningful continuation of their connection.

The Evening Unfolds

At 7:00 p.m., Mr. Right arrived. They enjoyed dinner filled with laughter and deep conversation, followed by a movie that allowed them to relax together.

They both felt it was one of their best evenings as the night ended. They cherished their connection and their journey.

Sunday: A Day of Worship and Rest

On Sunday, they attended church together. Ms. Right felt guided to join Mr. Right's church, finding a sense of belonging. After lunch, they decided to make their relationship exclusive, sharing a meaningful kiss on the cheek before parting.

They both felt content, ready to reflect and rest.

Chapter 6

The Cook

Monday: The Art of Communication

Ms. Right arrived at the Counselor's warm, inviting home that afternoon, her heart full of joy and excitement. She eagerly shared with the Counselor the details of how well her date with Mr. Right had unfolded and how she felt led to join his church on Sunday.

The Counselor congratulated her, expressing heartfelt happiness for her progress and the new chapter she was stepping into.

With the room filled with warmth and gratitude, the two prayed and transitioned to the purpose of the day: embarking on 'The Cook,' the sixth phase of the Experience.

As the Counselor stirred a pot in the kitchen, she explained how this phase would focus on preparing Ms. Right to create space for a healthy relationship built on mutual care and understanding.

After savoring the freshly prepared and delicious lunch together, they moved to the cozy living room. Settling on the couch, the Counselor handed Ms. Right a manual for the final two phases, smiling as she explained the importance of these last steps. The journey was coming full circle, and Ms. Right felt a deep sense of anticipation and readiness for the blessings that awaited her.

"This guide will help you navigate the next steps, but our next focus will be on one essential element—communication," the Counselor said. They agreed that open, honest dialogue was the foundation of lasting connection.

"Communication is the heartbeat of any relationship," the Counselor explained. Ms. Right left with a reminder that expressing herself openly, using words like "I feel," would strengthen her bond with others.

The day ended with prayer, thanking God for the insight gained and asking for continued wisdom in applying these lessons.

Reflecting Scripture:
"Let no corrupt communication proceed out of your mouth, but that which is good to the use of edifying, that it may minister grace unto the hearers." (Ephesians 4:29 KJV)

Tuesday: Embracing Self-Contentment

Ms. Right walked into the Counselor's warm and inviting home, feeling hopeful and energized. The comforting aroma of a freshly prepared meal filled the air, setting a peaceful and welcoming tone.

They enjoyed the delicious lunch together, sharing lighthearted conversation and laughter that deepened their connection. Before diving into the lesson, they paused and prayed, asking God for wisdom and guidance as they worked through the next step.

The Counselor then opened the manual to the topic of loneliness. She explained how loneliness, if not addressed, could lead to seeking validation in unfulfilling relationships. Together, they explored the importance of finding contentment within herself, leaning on God as her ultimate source of fulfillment.

This lesson reminded Ms. Right that embracing her singleness wasn't about waiting for someone else to complete her, but about cultivating wholeness and joy in her own journey with Christ.

"You are a beautiful work in progress," the Counselor reassured. Empowered by this insight, Ms. Right understood that this phase was about embracing her wholeness, not filling the void with someone else.

The day ended with prayer, thanking God for His presence and the strength to embrace her journey.

Reflecting Scripture:
"Not that I speak in respect of want: for I have learned, in whatsoever state I am, therewith to be content."
(Philippians 4:11 KJV)

Wednesday: Learning to Love Yourself

Ms. Right eagerly knocked on the Counselor's door, sunlight pouring into the cozy space where a lovingly prepared lunch awaited. They sat down to enjoy the meal, sharing heartfelt conversations that deepened their connection and set the tone for the lesson ahead.

After finishing the delicious lunch, they paused to pray, asking God for wisdom and guidance as they moved forward. With hearts prepared, the Counselor opened the manual to the next step—self-love. She explained that self-love was a crucial foundation for any healthy relationship, as it reflected understanding and embracing the love God has for each of His creations.

Through their discussion, Ms. Right began to see how nurturing self-love was an act of worship and preparation, allowing her to better serve and love others in the way God intended.

"Love is the most important ingredient in life," the Counselor began, "and it all starts with how you love yourself." She encouraged Ms. Right to nurture her self-love daily, reminding her that it forms the foundation for all other relationships.

Feeling inspired, Ms. Right left with a renewed commitment to cherish her own worth.

The day ended with prayer, asking God to teach her how to see herself through His eyes.

Reflecting Scripture:
"Thou shalt love thy neighbour as thyself." (Matthew 22:39 KJV)

Thursday: Enjoying Your Own Company
The day began with prayer, seeking joy and contentment in solitude.

Thursday brought a sense of peace as Ms. Right arrived. The Counselor had set a table for one, symbolizing the joy of solitude. She encouraged Ms. Right to view being alone as an opportunity for joyful independence and wholeness.

Ms. Right envisioned the meals she would enjoy by herself, savoring her own company and embracing the fullness of who she was in Christ.

The Counselor reinforced that solitude could be a beautiful gift, a time to reflect on being complete and whole within herself and in God.

The day ended with prayer, thanking God for the gift of peace in solitude and for teaching her to find wholeness and delight in her own company.

Reflecting Scripture:
"And ye are complete in him, which is the head of all principality and power." (Colossians 2:10 KJV)

Friday: Preparing for a Healthy Relationship

Ms. Right entered the Counselor's home with gratitude, eager to wrap up the week's lessons.

They enjoyed the delicious lunch together, reflecting on the progress Ms. Right had made and celebrating the transformation she was experiencing. Afterward, they paused to pray, asking God for continued guidance and wisdom as they delved into the day's lesson.

The Counselor explained that being 'The Cook' of her life meant creating space to receive a healthy relationship while also equipping herself with the tools to nurture and sustain it. This phase was about intentional preparation, ensuring that Ms. Right was ready to welcome and cultivate the blessings God had in store for her future.

As the message sank in, Ms. Right realized her journey wasn't just about finding love but preparing herself to maintain and embrace it fully.

The Counselor, proud of her growth, encouraged her to reflect on the self-awareness she had gained and the steps she would take to foster a lasting, fulfilling relationship.

The day ended with prayer, thanking God for equipping her with the tools to build a life rooted in faith and love.

Reflecting Scripture:
"And let us not be weary in well doing: for in due season we shall reap, if we faint not." (Galatians 6:9 KJV)

Saturday: Evaluating Progress

Mr. and Ms. Right returned to the Counselor's home for a warm, inviting lunch, ready to review the progress through 'The Cook.' The comforting aroma of the meal filled the room as they all sat down together, sharing laughter and conversation while enjoying the delicious food.

After the meal, they paused to pray, thanking God for the growth and insights gained during the week and inviting His presence into their reflections.

As they began reviewing the week's experiences, Mr. Right smiled and remarked, "It seems like you and the Counselor had another productive week," his excitement evident in his voice. His words filled the room with encouragement, reminding Ms. Right of how far she had come on her journey of preparation and transformation.

Ms. Right beamed, feeling supported and understood. The Counselor then introduced the final phase of the Experience, 'The Serve,' explaining that it was about learning to serve oneself first and embracing God's unique calling. This phase, they noted, would solidify everything Ms. Right worked on, helping her step into the fullness of a new relationship and individual purpose.

The day ended with prayer, thanking God for the journey so far, and asking for guidance in the final phase.

Sunday: Worship and Rest

On Sunday, Mr. and Ms. Right enjoyed worship and a relaxing lunch. They returned to their homes and spent the day resting and reflecting on their journey, eager to embrace the final chapter of Ms. Right's experience.

Chapter 7

The Serve

Monday: Embracing Purpose to Prepare for a Healthy Relationship

Ms. Right returned to the Counselor's home, feeling the importance of this final phase, "The Serve," in her journey. After a nourishing lunch, they prayed and settled on the couch, where many meaningful conversations occurred. The Counselor handed her a beautifully bound manual titled The Serve: Embracing Purpose to Prepare for a Healthy Relationship.

"This is your guide for this phase," the Counselor said warmly. "It's a map to help you embrace your God-given purpose and prepare for healthy relationships."

Ms. Right felt inspired as she opened the manual dedicated to her journey of self-discovery and love.

Seeking After Purpose: The Ingredients of Fulfillment

To serve others, you must first understand your purpose. God has uniquely designed you, and His Word guides you toward fulfilling that purpose. Ephesians 2:10kjv ("For we are his workmanship, created in Christ Jesus unto good works, which God hath before ordained that we should walk in them.") reminds us that we are created to do good works.

Reflect on your natural skills and passions. God has given you these tools to serve Him and find true fulfillment, which goes beyond external validation.

Serving Your Gifts: Offering Back to God

"Serving your gifts" means using your talents as worship. True fulfillment comes from serving God's mission, not seeking relationship validation. Romans 12:1kjv ("I beseech you therefore, brethren, by the mercies of God, that ye present your bodies a living sacrifice, holy, acceptable unto God, which is your reasonable service.") encourages us to offer ourselves to God, shifting our focus from relationship status to our relationship with Christ.

When rooted in Christ, you won't feel incomplete. Instead, you'll find confidence and joy in fulfilling His will.

Releasing the Spirit of Neediness: Rooting Yourself in Christ

Letting go of neediness is crucial. Our desire for relationships can lead to feelings of incompleteness, but knowing you are whole in Christ frees you from anxiety. Ephesians 3:19kjv ("And to know the love of Christ that surpasses knowledge, that you may be filled with all the fullness of God.") reminds us of His love, which surpasses all understanding.

As you embrace God's love, you will rest in your worth and stop seeking validation elsewhere.

Allowing the Word to Penetrate: Remembering Who You Are in Christ

Daily practices like prayer and studying Scripture will help you stay aligned with your identity in Christ. James 1:22kjv ("But be ye doers of the word, and not hearers only, deceiving your own selves.") urges us to be doers of the Word, reflecting our true selves.

Remember that you are wonderfully made and equipped for every good work. This understanding builds confidence that no relationship can provide and prepares you to serve joyfully.

Busy Serving, Patiently Waiting: The Fruit of Purposeful Living
Focusing on serving your purpose shifts your attention away from waiting for relationships. Psalm 37:4kjv ("Delight thyself also in the Lord: and he shall give thee the desires of thine heart.") encourages us to delight in the Lord; in doing so, we will find joy and patience.

Serving God brings fulfillment that helps you wait for His timing in all areas of life, including relationships.

www.ingramcontent.com/pod-product-compliance
Lightning Source LLC
Chambersburg PA
CBHW071934240426
43668CB00038B/1799